S0-BRZ-029

# Anthems
# for Choirs
# 4

26 anthems for mixed voices
by twentieth-century composers

## Compiled by
## CHRISTOPHER MORRIS

# Oxford University Press

Music Department    Walton Street    Oxford    OX2 6DP

© Oxford University Press 1976

*Not for sale in the United States of America*

Printed in Great Britain

## Preface

These twenty-six anthems by twentieth-
century composers have been chosen
to suit cathedrals, collegiate churches,
and those parish churches supporting
cathedral-type choirs, but many of the
anthems will be found useful to average
parish-church choirs.

Two anthems have been written especially
for this book by Kenneth Leighton and
Alan Ridout.

The collection covers all the main seasons
and festivals of the Church's Year, and
also includes a number of anthems for
general use. Twelve of the anthems are
suitable for unaccompanied singing.

# Index of Titles and First Lines

*Where first lines differ from titles the former are shown in italics*

Anthems suitable for unaccompanied singing are marked thus *

# Seasonal Index

# Index of Composers

# 1. O THOU THE CENTRAL ORB

H. R. BRAMLEY
(1833 – 1917)

CHARLES WOOD
(1866 – 1926)

Copyright 1915 The Year Book Press

Reprinted by permission of Ascherberg, Hopwood & Crew Ltd.

-perse the gloom of sin, Our na-ture all shall
-perse the gloom of sin, Our na-ture all shall
-perse the gloom of sin, Our na-ture all shall
-perse the gloom of sin, Our na-ture all shall

Ped.

feel e-ter-nal day, In fel-low-ship with
feel e-ter-nal day, In fel-low-ship with
feel e-ter-nal day, In fel-low-ship with
feel e-ter-nal day, In fel-low-ship with

Man.

*Commissioned by the Cardiff Polyphonic Choir in association with the Welsh Arts Council.*

# 2. PUER NATUS

16th c. German words
Tr. W. Moelwyn Merchant

ALUN HODDINOTT

This anthem may be sung by mixed voices, or sopranos and altos, or tenors and basses. It is also published separately (X 229).

© Oxford University Press 1972

# 3. ON THIS DAY EARTH SHALL RING

Words from an old Swedish Carol

H. C. STEWART

This anthem is published separately (A 64).

Copyright Oxford University Press 1934

save us, Him the Fa - ther gave us, I - de - o, I - de - o, I - de - o.

Glo - ri - a, Glo - ri - a in ex - cel - sis De - o.

2 His the doom, ours the mirth, When He came down to earth, Beth - le - hem saw His
3 God's bright star, o'er His head, Wise men three to Him led, Kneel they low by His

song earth shall ring Praising Christ, Heaven's King.    Born on earth to    save us,

Peace and love He    gave____ us, I - de - o,    I - de - o,    I - de - o.

Glo - ri - a, Glo - ri - a    in __ ex - cel - sis De - o.

# 4. LORD, THOU HAST TOLD US

THOMAS WASHBOURNE
(1606 – 1687)

ARNOLD BAX
(1883 – 1953)

Copyright 1931 Oxford University Press

From *Enlarged Songs of Praise* by permission of Oxford University Press.

# 5. A LITANY

PHINEAS FLETCHER
(1582 – 1650)

WILLIAM WALTON

This anthem is published separately (OCS 733).

Copyright Oxford University Press 1930

# 6. CHRIST THE LORD IS RISEN AGAIN

Words by MICHAEL WEISSE (c. 1480–1534)
tr. CATHERINE WINKWORTH

JOHN RUTTER

This anthem is published separately (E 124).

© Oxford University Press 1971

18

bro - ken    ev - 'ry    chain! _____
us    en - dur'd    the    strife, _____

24  *mf*

Hark,    the    an - gels    shout    for    joy, _____
Is    our    Pas - chal    Lamb    to - day!

30    *cresc.*

____ Sing - ing    ev - er -    more ___    on    high,
We    too    sing    for    joy, ___    and    say

35    S.  *f*
      A.
Al - le - lu - ia,    al - le - lu - ia,    al - le - lu - ia,    al -
      T.
35    B.  *f*

Ch. or Gt. *f*

Ped.

*2nd soprano part here and elsewhere may be omitted, if necessary.

*Commissioned for the St. Albans Diocesan Choirs Festival 1974*

# 7. LIFT UP YOUR HEADS

JOSEPH BEAUMONT
(1615–1699)

FRANCIS JACKSON
(Opus 44, No. 2)

© Oxford University Press 1976

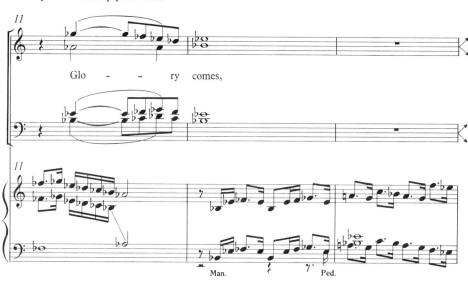

Glo - - ry comes,

and Glo - ry's King;

and Glo - ry's King;

and Glo - ry's King;

and Glo - ry's King;

meno

Now by your high all-gold-en way    The fair-er

Now by your high all-gold-en way The fair — — er

Now by your high all-gold-en way    The fair-er

Now by your high all-gold-en way The fair — — er

Heaven comes home to-day._____

Heaven comes home,    comes home to-day.

Heaven comes home,    comes home_____ to-day.

Heaven comes home,    comes home_____ to-day.

*for Lionel Dakers*
*and the Incorporated Association of Organists*

# 8. O CLAP YOUR HANDS

Psalm 47, vv. 1–7

JOHN RUTTER

This anthem is published separately (A 307).

It has been scored for double woodwind, 2 hns., 2 tpts., percussion, hp., and strings.   Scores and parts are on hire.

Ⓒ Oxford University Press 1973

# 9. A PURE RIVER OF WATER OF LIFE

CHRISTINA ROSETTI
(1830 – 1894)

ALAN RIDOUT

© Oxford University Press 1976

*For Mairi Rolland and The Kinghorn Singers*
*to celebrate their 21st anniversary*

# 10. A HYMN TO THE TRINITY

Anon.

KENNETH LEIGHTON

© Oxford University Press 1976

★The bass line in brackets is *ad lib.*

God and per- sons three, ___ one God and per- sons three; ___

God and per- sons three, one God and per- sons three; ___

God and per- sons three, one God and per- sons three; ___

God and per- sons three, one God and per- sons three; ___

___ As it is, ___ as it is now, ___

As it is, ___ as it is now, ___

As it is, ___ as it is

As it is,

As it is,

*Composed for the marriage of H.R.H. The Princess Elizabeth*
*and Lieutenant Philip Mountbatten R.N. in*
*Westminster Abbey on 20 November 1947*

# 11. WE WAIT FOR THY LOVING KINDNESS

Words selected by
the Rev. C. M. ARMITAGE,
Precentor of Westminster

WILLIAM McKIE

We wait for thy loving kind - ness, O God: in the midst of thy

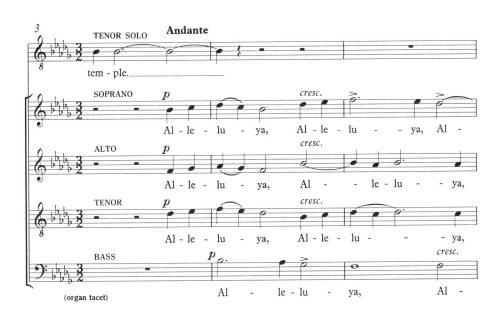

This anthem is published separately (A 124).

Copyright Oxford University Press 1947

*Dedicated to the Honourable Ivor Guest and the Lady Mabel Fox-Strangways*
*on the occasion of their marriage, Nov. 22nd, 1938.*

# 12. SET ME AS A SEAL

From the Song of Solomon

WILLIAM WALTON

This anthem is published separately (A 86).

Copyright Oxford University Press 1938

*Composed for the Coronation of Her Majesty Queen Elizabeth II*
*in Westminster Abbey on 2 June 1953*

# 13. O TASTE AND SEE

Psalm 34, v. 8

R. VAUGHAN WILLIAMS
(1872—1958)

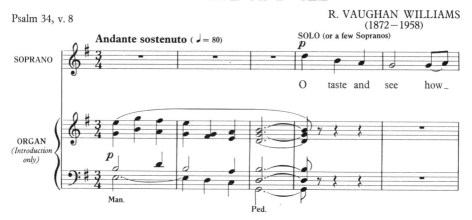

This anthem may be sung in the key of G flat. It is also published separately (A 349).

Copyright Oxford University Press 1953

# 14. LET ALL MORTAL FLESH KEEP SILENCE

Words from the Liturgy of St. James

EDWARD C. BAIRSTOW
(1874—1946)

★If found too high for male altos, these notes may be omitted, or the anthem may be sung in F minor.

By permission of Stainer & Bell, Ltd. Copyright 1925

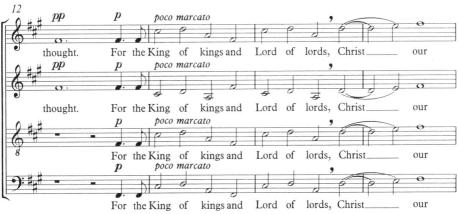

# 15. THOU, O GOD, ART PRAISED IN SION

Verses from Psalm 65

IAN HARE

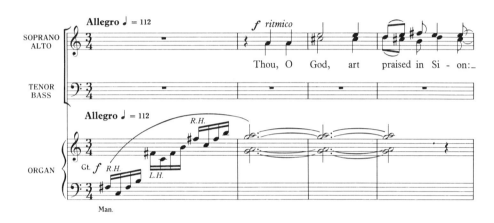

Note: In the first two phrases the Alto part may be sung by 2nd Sopranos.

© Oxford University Press 1973

*Affectionately dedicated to Sir Hugh Allen*

# 16. FAIRE IS THE HEAVEN

EDMUND SPENSER
(1553 — 1599)

WILLIAM H. HARRIS
(1883 — 1973)

Copyright 1925 by The Year Book Press (revised 1948). Reprinted by permission of Ascherberg, Hopwood & Crew Ltd.

Whence they— doe still be - hold the glo — rious

Whence they— doe still be - hold the glo — —

Whence they— doe still be-hold the glo — rious

Whence they doe still be-hold the glo — —

- li - ci-tie;

- li - ci-tie;

- li - ci-tie;

- li - ci-tie;

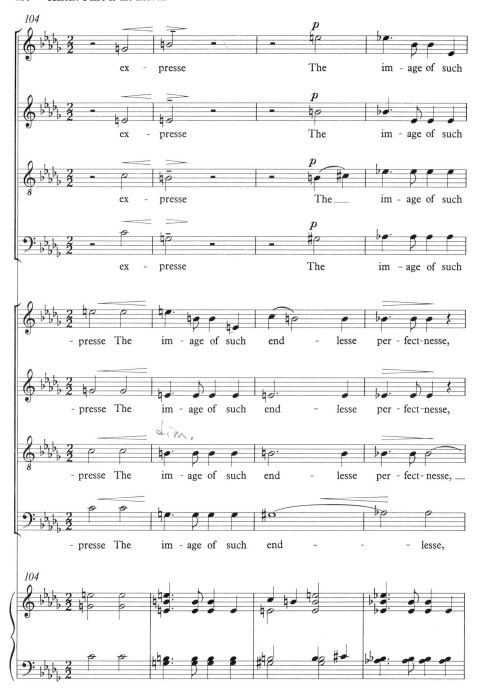

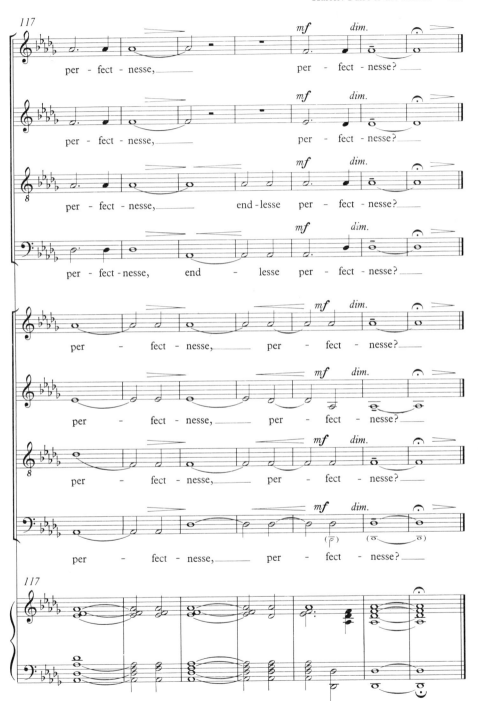

# 17. GIVE US THE WINGS OF FAITH

ISAAC WATTS
(1674–1748)

ERNEST BULLOCK

This anthem is published separately (A 1)

Copyright Oxford University Press 1925

*Dedicated to the Very Reverend Gwynno James on the occasion of his*
*Installation as Dean of Brecon 17 October 1964*

# 18. MAKE A JOYFUL NOISE
## *(JUBILATE DEO)*

Psalm 100

WILLIAM MATHIAS
Op. 26, No. 2

This anthem is published separately (A 220).

© Oxford University Press 1965

God:_____ it is he that hath made us, and

*poco a poco dim.*

not__ we__ our - selves:_____ it is he that hath made us, and

not__ we__ our - selves:_____ we are his peo - ple, and the

(Ped.)

*Written for St. George's Chapel, Windsor, at the request of H.R.H. The Duke of Edinburgh*

# 19. O BE JOYFUL IN THE LORD
## (JUBILATE DEO)

Psalm 100

BENJAMIN BRITTEN

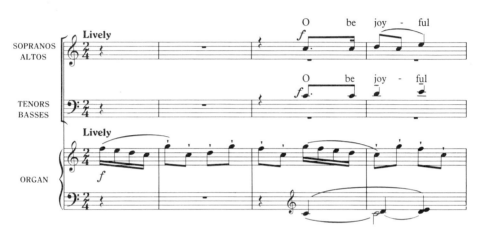

This anthem is published by arrangement with Messrs. Boosey & Hawkes Ltd. It is also available separately (OUP S551).

© Oxford University Press 1961

42
and speak good of his name.
and speak good_ of his name.
42
pp
47
sust.
For the Lord is gra - cious,_
sust.
For the Lord is gra - cious,_
47

Aldeburgh, Feb. 1961

*to F.F.*

# 20. O HOW AMIABLE

From psalms 84 and 90

R. VAUGHAN WILLIAMS
(1872–1958)

This anthem is published separately (A 94).

Copyright Oxford University Press 1940

swal - low a nest where she may lay her young:_____ ev - en thy

al - tars, O Lord of_ hosts,_____ my King_ and my

God._____ Bless - ed are they that dwell in thy_ house:_____

they will be al - way prais - ing thee.

Poco più mosso ( ♩ = 100)    S. & A. *ff*

The glo - rious ma-jes - ty of the

T. & B.

*ff*

*f* *sostenuto*

Lord our God be up - on us: pros - per thou the work of our

**54**

**57** *ff* Voices in unison

O God, our help in a - ges past, Our

**63**

hope for years to come, Our shel - ter from the

**69** S. & T. *ff*

A. & B.

storm - y blast, And our e - ter - nal home.

*ff*

*To Sir Thomas Armstrong*

# 21. LIKE AS THE HART

Psalm 42, vv. 1 – 3

HERBERT HOWELLS

This anthem is published separately (A 109).

Copyright Oxford University Press 1943

*For the Choristers of New College, Oxford*

## 22. JESU DULCIS MEMORIA

11th-century words

PAUL DRAYTON

© Oxford University Press 1970

su — — — — — per mel,    su — per mel et

Su — per mel,    su — per mel    et

Su — — — — per mel,    su — per mel et

- cun-di-us,    Nil co - gi - ta - tur dul-ci-us,    co — gi — tatur __

om — ni - a,    Je — — su De — i

om — ni - a, __    Je — su De - i    Fi — — —

om — ni - a, __    Je — su    De — i    Fi —

__ dul — ci-us    Quam Je - su De — i

Je - su dul - cis me - mo - ri - a_____    Dans ve - ra  cor - di

aah_____

(molto legato)  aah_____

aah_____

aah_____

gau - di - a, _____    Sed su - per mel et  om - ni - a,

mm_____

aah_____

mm_____

(molto legato)

mm_____    mm_____

*For the choir of Coventry Cathedral*

# 23. A PRAYER FOR PEACE

Anon. (c. 1500)

DAVID LORD

If it is desired to lengthen the work bars 1—16 may be repeated.

© Oxford University Press 1971

# 24. GREATER LOVE HATH NO MAN

JOHN IRELAND
(1879 – 1962)

†Song of Solomon viii, 7 & 6

By permission of Stainer & Bell, Ltd.  Copyright 1912

non legato

†St. John xv, 13

SOPRANO SOLO

†Who his own self bare our sins in his own bo - dy on the tree, that we, be - ing dead to sins, should live un - to right - eous-ness,

senza Ped.

Ped.

senza Ped.

Ped.

BARITONE SOLO
*mf caldamente*

that we, be - ing dead to sins, should

cresc.

senza Ped.

†I Peter ii, 24

† I Corinthians vi, 11

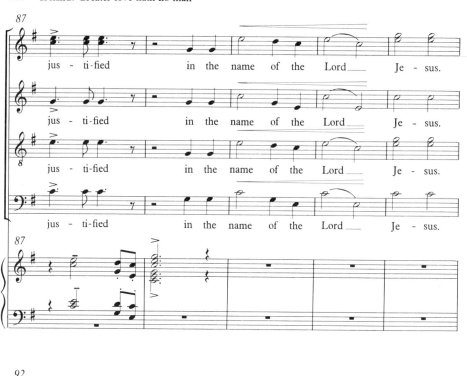

†I Peter ii, 9

# 25. TURN BACK, O MAN

CLIFFORD BAX
(1886–1962)

GUSTAV HOLST
(1874–1934)

*Melody ('The Old 124th Psalm') from the Genevan Psalter

By permission of Stainer & Bell, Ltd. Copyright 1919

Nor till that hour shall God's whole will be done.

Now, e-ven now,___ once___ more from earth to sky___

# 26. O CLAP YOUR HANDS

From Psalm 47

R. VAUGHAN WILLIAMS
(1872–1958)

The original version of the accompaniment for 3 trumpets, 3 trombones, tuba (*ad lib.*), timpani, cymbals (*ad lib.*), and organ is on hire from Stainer and Bell Ltd.

By permission of Stainer & Bell Ltd. Copyright 1920

Processed and printed by
Halstan & Co. Ltd., Amersham, Bucks., England